HARDPRESS.NET

ISBN: 9781314295269

Published by:
HardPress Publishing
8345 NW 66TH ST #2561
MIAMI FL 33166-2626

Email: info@hardpress.net
Web: http://www.hardpress.net

Popular Studies in Mythology, Romance and Folklore

ISSUED UNDER THE GENERAL EDITORSHIP OF

MR. ALFRED NUTT

PAST PRESIDENT OF THE FOLKLORE SOCIETY
AUTHOR OF "STUDIES ON THE LEGEND OF THE HOLY GRAIL" AND "THE VOYAGE OF BRAN"

Each 16mo. 6d. net (7d. post free)

This series is intended to impart, in a concise and accurate but thoroughly popular manner, information concerning the subjects of which it treats. Each study gives a broad survey of the theme, unembarrassed by notes or references. Bibliographical appendices are provided for those who wish to carry the study of these subjects further.

The Editor ventures to point out that *nowhere else* can the English reader obtain information given in a concise and popular form, yet based upon and in accordance with the latest researches of scholarship concerning the subjects of which the Series treats. He also ventures to call attention to the fact that the most favourable notices of the Popular Studies are those due to the learned press of the Continent and America.

Ossian and the Ossianic Literature

By

Alfred Nutt

Author of "The Voyage of Bran" (Essays on the Irish Vision of the Happy Otherworld and The Celtic Doctrine of Rebirth)

SECOND EDITION

Published by David Nutt, at the Sign of the Phœnix, Long Acre, London

1910

PREFACE

In preparing a revised edition of the present study I have, deliberately, refrained from more than a minimum of change. The work done in the last ten years does not, in my opinion, necessitate any substantial modification of the picture I drew in 1899 *which, itself, was the outcome of my studies of* 1889–1892. *I have given* (*pp.* 27–30) *an account of what has been issued so far, of the only important new Ossianic Material, Mr. MacNeill's edition of the Duanaire Finn. Were the whole, instead of a portion merely of the Duanaire accessible some of my views concerning the dates and relative relationships of sections of Ossianic literature might require modification, but judging by what has been published, I see no reason for doubting the substantial accuracy of the scheme of development which I have outlined.*

Mr. MacNeill's theory of the true nature and origins of the Ossianic cycle stands on a different footing. Were I convinced of its correctness I should have given another shape to certain portions of this study, have emphasised features I have left in the shade, have traced other lines along which to follow the development of the cycle. But greatly as I admire Mr. MacNeill's constructive scholarship, warmly as I welcome the light he has thrown upon certain features of Ossianic literature, I cannot feel that he has made out his case. I have therefore contented myself with summarising his contentions in an appendix (pp. 53–60), *and with briefly indicating my grounds for agreement or dissent.*

I have left unaltered the words of advice which, in 1899, *I addressed to students desirous of advancing the interpretation of Ossianic legend by original work. So far they have been entirely neglected in both sections of Gaeldom. The School of Irish Learning established in the interval naturally and rightly directed the attention of its students in the first place to older and less known sections of Irish literature; it may, however, be hoped that Professor Bergin will set some of his pupils to work on Ossianic texts. Further, the new Irish University should bring into the field a number of enthusiastic and scientifically trained students. Should a new edition of this study be called for at my hands, I trust I may have to record substantial advance in our knowledge and appreciation of every section of Ossianic literature.*

ALFRED NUTT

OSSIAN AND THE OSSIANIC LITERATURE

"WOODY MORVEN and echoing Sora, and Selma with its silent halls!—we all owe them a debt of gratitude, and when we are unjust enough to forget it, may the Muse forget us!"

These words of Matthew Arnold's fairly reflect the feelings towards Ossian and the literature connected with his name of such cultivated Englishmen as concern themselves at all with the subject, their knowledge of it is derived from James Macpherson; their appreciation depends upon whether or no they share Arnold's admiration for the undoubted beauties of his remarkable work; their attitude towards the critical questions involved differs but little from that of the combatants in the great critical battle urged a century ago over the authenticity of the so-called Ossian. As the following pages ignore Macpherson altogether, I must briefly state the opinion held of his work by most competent scholars. He undoubtedly had some knowledge of the Ossianic ballad literature existing in the Highlands in his day, and he worked up many of its themes into his English Ossian, which is, however, almost as much his own composition as "Paradise Lost" is the composition of Milton. He suffered himself to maintain the existence of a Gaelic original which he claimed to have rendered faithfully; one was published many years later, but it is probably a mere retranslation into Gaelic of the English Ossian. For the student, whether of Celtic myth and saga, of Celtic archæology, or of Gaelic style and literary form, Macpherson's poems are worthless; they disregard the traditional versions of the legends, they depart from the traditional representation of the material life depicted in the old and genuine texts, and they utterly ignore the traditional conventions of Gaelic style. But Macpherson's flashes of genuine inspiration, and the importance of his work in preparing the romantic movement of the nineteenth century, will always secure for him a high place on the roll of Scottish writers.

Who then is the Ossian and what the Ossianic literature that form the subject of the following pages? It will be convenient to take the latter question first.

The body of Gaelic literature connected with the name of Ossian is of very considerable extent and of respectable antiquity. The oldest texts, prose for the most part, but also in verse, are preserved in Irish

MSS. of the eleventh and twelfth centuries, and go back to a period from 150 to 250 years older at least. The bulk of Ossianic literature is, however, of later date as far as the form under which it has come down to us is concerned. A number of important texts, prose for the most part, are preserved in MSS. of the fourteenth and fifteenth centuries, but were probably redacted in the thirteenth and twelfth centuries. But by far the largest mass consists of narrative poems, as a rule dramatic in structure. These have come down to us in MSS. written in Scotland from the end of the fifteenth to the middle of the seventeenth century, in Ireland from the sixteenth down to the middle of the present century. The Gaelic speaking peasantry, alike in Ireland and Scotland, have preserved orally a large number of these ballads, as also a great mass of prose narratives, the heroes of which are Ossian and his comrades. A rough classification may be made into (*a*) pre-mediæval texts (vouched for by MSS. of the twelfth century and earlier), (*b*) mediæval (MSS. of the fourteenth and fifteenth centuries) and (*c*) post mediæval texts. Whilst there are marked differences in style and tone between the different sections, as well as between the specific Irish and Scotch versions of the third section, this body of literature is on the whole wonderfully homogeneous; themes, characterisation, personages, *locale*, have undergone scarce any change from the eleventh century to the present day.

Were all Ossianic texts preserved in MSS. older than the present century to be printed they would fill some eight to ten thousand 8vo pages. The mere bulk of the literature, even if we allow for considerable repetition of incident, arrests attention. If we further recall that for the last five hundred years this body of romance has formed the chief imaginative recreation of Gaeldom, alike in Ireland and Scotland, and that a peasantry unable to read or write has yet preserved it almost entire, its claims to consideration and study will appear manifest. No literature can, for so many centuries, maintain itself and preserve its plastic vitality without good and sufficient reason. An endeavour to realise the nature of the appeal which this literature made and still makes to the Gaelic race at once brings us to the question—is it wholly a work of imagination, or has it preserved, in howsoever fanciful a form, some record of historic fact? And thus we are led back to our starting-point—who were Ossian, and the heroes associated with him?

If we turn to the Irish annals we find that Oisín (the proper spelling of the name phonetically transcribed Ossian by Macpherson, a transcription which I retain for convenience' sake) was the son of Finn mac Cumhail, who is asserted to have been the leader of a band of professional soldiers and to have lived in the third century of our era. Irish historical writers of the tenth and eleventh centuries record Finn's death, some in 252, some in 283. In so far as an historical thread connects the scattered episodes of the cycle, it is to be found in the rivality between Finn's band (the Clanna Baoisgne) and the Clanna Morna of which Goll was leader, and in the relations of both bodies to the internecine feuds of the Irish kings. Finn is represented as quarrelling with Cormac, son of Art, the most famous high-king in Irish legend, whose daughter, Grainne, he had married, and the feud thus formed was carried on by the children, culminating ultimately in the battle of Gabhra, in which Cairbre, Cormac's son, and Finn's grandson, Oscar, son of Ossian, the Achilles of the cycle, fell at each other's hands. The Fenian host perished almost to the last man in this battle, only a few surviving, with miraculously prolonged life, until the coming of Patrick two centuries later.

How far can this legendary history be accepted as in any sense a genuine record of events? In the first place we must note that it was firmly believed in by Irish historical writers of the eleventh century, men fully abreast of all the learning of their time, by no means devoid of the critical instinct and in possession of great masses of tribal tradition and genealogical record which have perished; on the other hand they lived centuries after the alleged events, they differ considerably among themselves as to the chronology of the cycle, and they were, like all men of the middle ages, unable to examine tradition critically as we moderns do. Fortunately there is little need for me to discuss the credibility or otherwise of the historic records concerning Finn, his family and his band of warriors. They may be accepted or rejected according to individual bent of mind without really modifying our view of the literature. For when we turn to the romances, whether in prose or verse, we find that, although the history is professedly the same as that of the annals, firstly we are transported to a world entirely romantic, in which divine and semi-divine beings, ungainly monsters and giants play a prominent part, in which men and women change shapes with animals, in which the lives of the heroes are miraculously prolonged—in short, we find ourselves in a land of Faery; secondly, we find that the historic conditions in which the heroes are represented as living do not for the most part answer to anything we know or can surmise of the third century. For Finn and his warriors are perpetually on the watch to guard Ireland against the attacks of oversea-raiders, styled Lochlannach by the narrators and by them undoubtedly thought of as Norsemen. But the latter, as is well known, only came to Ireland at the close of the eighth century, and the heroic period of their invasions extended for about a century, from 825 to 925; to be followed by a period of comparative settlement during the tenth century, until at the opening of the eleventh century the battle of Clontarf, fought by Brian, the great South Irish chieftain, marked the break-up of the separate Teutonic organisation and the absorption of the Teutons into the fabric of Irish life. In these pages then we may disregard the otherwise interesting question of historic credibility in the Ossianic romances: firstly, because they have their being in a land unaffected by fact; secondly, because if they ever did reflect the history of the third century, the reflection was distorted in after times, and a pseudo-history based upon events of the ninth and tenth centuries was substituted for it. What the historian seeks for in legend is far more a picture of the society in which it took rise than a record of the events which it commemorates. We shall see presently what traces, if any, of third-century custom and manners are preserved by extant texts of the Ossianic cycle.*

(*a*) Pre-mediæval Ossianic Romance.

The pre-mediæval remains of the cycle, contained

* In the Appendix, pp. 53–60, I discuss Mr. MacNeill's views respecting the racial and historical origins of the cycle.

in MSS. copied in the twelfth and eleventh centuries from earlier MSS., though not very numerous, are yet numerous enough to furnish prototypes of well-nigh every mode of conceiving the character and presenting the fortunes of the heroes which we find in the modern texts. All the texts which we know definitely to be older than the twelfth century would probably not fill more than one hundred pages, but these hundred pages contain in germ the many thousand pages of the mediæval and post-mediæval literature. These early fragments of the legends (it is seldom we get more than a fragment) are every whit as "romantic" as the later tales and ballads. Indeed the further back we trace these Fenian tales, the more markedly mythical do we find them. A remarkable tale contained in the oldest Irish profane MS., the Book of the Dun Cow, and probably as old as the eighth century, brings Finn, supposed to have died in the third century, to life again as a sixth-century Ulster Kinglet, Mongan. Finn-Mongan has a dispute with Dallan Forgall, chief bard of Ireland, concerning some event of the third century. To substantiate his contention he calls up from the other world Caoilte mac Ronain, the fleetest foot among the Fenian heroes, whose testimony, in favour of the king, is accepted as final. Another long poem, entitled Finn and the Phantoms, tells how Finn in company with Caoilte and Ossian, after outriding their companions whilst hunting, came at nightfall to a house of whose existence in that district they knew nothing. They were received by a grey giant, a hag with three heads on her thin neck, and a headless man with one eye in his breast; nine bodies rise on one side of the house, nine on the other, and raise nine harsh shrieks—"Not melodious was that concert." The hideous crew attack the heroes, who are sore put to it to defend themselves until sunlight, when the tribe of monsters falls dead on the spot. Again another tale tells how the Fianna of Melgi chase and kill Aige transformed into a deer.

Some of these pre-mediæval texts are specially noteworthy in view of their relation to the later romances. Thus one long poem, put into Finn's mouth, employs that favourite device of Irish story-telling, topographical enumeration; the mention of hills, or streams, or burial mounds, calls forth the appropriate legend for each. As we shall see presently, one of the most important of the later texts is built upon this model. Another poem, also ascribed to Finn, strikes a note which remains dominant throughout the entire range of Ossianic literature, the note of keen and vivid feeling for certain natural conditions. It is a brief description of winter:

"A tale here for you, oxen lowing, winter's snowing, summer's passing; wind from the north, high and cold, low the sun and short his course, wildly tossing the wave of the sea. The fern burns deep red. Men wrap themselves closely, the wild goose raises her wonted cry, cold seizes the wing of the bird; 'tis the season of ice; sad my tale!"

A poem ascribed to Caoilte anticipates a very common theme in the later romances. Three strange hunters come oversea bringing with them a hound of the King of Hiruatha (*i.e.* Norway); they slay one of Finn's men, Duban, and the Fianna demand their death, but Finn declares he will accept the hound as compensation. After pledging themselves thereto by sun and moon and sea and earth, the strangers kill the dog and fly, carrying its hide with them, to the north-east, passing Scotland on the way. The Fianna assemble in pursuit and heap up a cairn before starting, each man flinging a stone upon it, whilst old and young swear that they will not retreat until the stone retreat for dread of the foreigners.

Finally the following poem, which is ascribed to Caoilte and figures him as surviving until the time of the Talcend (*i.e.* Patrick, according to a gloss in the MS.), embodies the most famous and characteristic *motif* of Ossianic legend, that which differentiates it from all other bodies of mythic and heroic romance. The hero, in his supernaturally prolonged old age, thus laments the glories of his youth and prime:

Small to-night the vigour of my feet,
I know my body is flesh;
Good was the running of my feet
Until the Talcend came.

Swift were my feet,
In my head my eyes kept ward,
My arms were wont to feed the carrion crow,
My weapons ne'er lacked a shout of victory.

. . . . .

I and Oisin, the son of Finn,
In unison we dealt our blows.
Mighty in sooth were our feats,
Small the boast we made of them.

In 1871, the Rev. J. G. Campbell picked up in Tiree a fragmentary lament for Caoilte, ascribed to Ossian, which runs thus:

Sorrowful am I after Caoilte,
Since my contemporaries are not alive.
I am filled with sadness, agony, and pain
At parting with my foster brother,
Caoilte, my true foster-brother,
With whom I could win victory and banner;
Caoilte, my perfect fellow-warrior,
A relief to the Fians in time of need.

The one poem is at least a thousand years old, the other still lives on the lips of the Gaelic peasant, but in tone, sentiment, expression they might be contemporary.

Attention has already been drawn to certain aspects of the pre-mediæval Ossianic legend, as presented in texts which must, as we have seen, be at least older than the twelfth century and which may belong in part to a period several centuries earlier. I will now recapitulate those features upon which, for the purposes of this study, I lay special stress. The chief heroes of the legend are Finn himself, his son Ossian and his sister's son Caoilte; the latter is pre-eminently the witness to, and relater of the mighty deeds achieved by himself and his fellow warriors; he, it is, who comes back from the other world to corroborate Finn, re-incarnated as Mongan and living three centuries and a half after the period assigned to him in the annals; he lives on until the days of Patrick and laments his departed strength and his lost comrades. But Ossian also shares this characteristic of supernaturally prolonged life and keen regret for vanished youth; the poem which describes the visit of the three heroes to the Phantoms introduces him as Guaire the blind, contrasting his sad lot with that of his hearers, and it is not until late in the poem that the blind minstrel reveals his identity with the famous son of Finn. Thus the earliest texts of the cycle represent it as miraculously preserved for the edification and delight of after ages; from the outset the legend, thrown back into the past, comes before the Gael as a tale of—

The old days that seem to be
Much older than any history
That is written in any book—

and breathes a note of lament and protest. From the outset too we find ourselves in a land of wizardry and shape shifting, a land which even the earliest hearers and tellers of those tales must have felt to be unreal. For the warriors who dwell in this land the chase is of scarce less moment than warfare, they engage in hunts which lead to a realm of glamour and illusion, they come and go over Northern Seas, receiving visits from and paying visits to the far off Scandinavian lands. As is but natural this hunter race is sensitive to the passing moods of Nature, and to the ways of the wild animals they chase.

Besides Caoilte and Ossian, the pre-eminent heroes, after Finn himself, of the earliest texts, we hear of Oscar falling at Gabhra, Oscar whose later fame excels that of any other hero. Goll too, the hard-smiting chief of the Clanna Morna, and Fergus, the poet of the warrior band, are mentioned, as is also another sister's son of Finn Diarmaid hua Duibne. A tenth-century commentator upon an obscure poem of the previous century, has preserved a verse which justifies the conclusion that the famous story of Diarmaid's elopement with Grainne, the wife of Finn, is as old as any portion of the cycle. The commentator quotes the verse as follows: "As Granne daughter of Cormac, said to Find—

"There lives a man
On whom I would love to gaze long,
For whom I would give the whole world,
O Son of Mary! though a privation!"

The allusion is undoubtedly to Grainne's love for Diarmaid. In the Fenian as in the Arthurian legend the passion of the chief hero's wife for his nephew forms an original and essential element. Here let me note that if the single verse, preserved by a luçky chance, be a fair specimen of the poem ascribed to Grainne and certainly not later than the end of the tenth century, it must have expressed the passion of love with a keen intensity unknown in any contemporary vernacular European literature.

(*b*) Mediæval Ossianic Romance.

I have briefly sketched the Ossianic literature preserved in the earliest Irish MSS. and undoubtedly older than the twelfth century. The whole may, as I have said, fill some hundred pages of modern print. It can only be a small portion of what was current at the time in Gaeldom; bits and scraps are all that is vouchsafed to us, scarce anything pretending to the name of a saga, a rounded sequence of incidents. Yet something of the kind must have existed or we cannot explain the presence of the Ossianic texts in the early MSS. For these, compiled as they were for kings and great chiefs, are libraries, containing everything in the way of history, sacred and profane, legend, national and foreign, and didactic teaching with which it was thought essential for a great man to be acquainted. The compilers reflected the literary and scholastic fashion of their day. The admission of the texts I have cited proves the existence of a body of Ossianic romance which must by the eleventh century have won some recognition from the bardic class; the small space accorded to it in comparison with that assigned to the other cycles of mythic and heroic saga, notably to the Ulster cycle of Conchobor and Cuchulinn, proves that it was far less fashionable than they. Turn now to MSS. compiled after the twelfth century and we note a great change. The proportion of Ossianic texts increases steadily from century to century until at last more than sixty per cent. of native Irish fiction is Ossianic or pseudo-Ossianic. We can, I think, explain this fact as due to historic causes of a perfectly definite nature, the consideration of which sheds a deal of light upon Irish literature at large. From the fourth down to the end of the tenth century the head kingship of Ireland had remained almost exclusively in the North Irish tribe of the Hy Neill, the descendants of Niall of the Nine Hostages. Pre-eminence was thus secured for the Northern traditions whether historical or mythical; the great heroic cycle of Ireland was that which commemorates the deeds of the Ulster chieftain Conchobor, of the Ulster braves Cuchulinn and Conall Cearnach. These traditions, these sagas, reflecting as they do the recitations of countless generations of storytellers and minstrels who had been accustomed to find the chief market for their wares among the dominant northern chieftains, make up the bulk of the great vellum MSS. which give us a fairly faithful idea of Irish literature up to the eleventh century. But at the beginning of that century a Munster chieftain, Brian of the Dalg Cais, wrested the head kingship of Ireland from the Hy Neill. The leading poets of the eleventh century were attached to the court of Brian and his descendants; a number of important historical and legal works emanated from Munster. Is it too bold an hypothesis that Brian's success gave to the Ossianic saga, which belongs essentially to the south of Ireland, a share in the pre-eminence which had previously been enjoyed by the northern heroic traditions? The Fenian tales existed long before the time of Brian, but they were not fashionable, they did not attract the attention of the chief bards and storytellers.

Munster's head kingship gave them a status and impcrtance which they had previously lacked.

This hypothesis explains much. As the Ossianic legends only came largely into the hands of the bardic and story-telling class centuries after the alleged date of their personages, they necessarily lack the firmer and more precise historic note which characterises the Ulster cycle, connected as that was from its very inception with a definite historical tradition. The action of the one cycle, the Northern, takes place on earth, many as may be its links with the land of gods and demons; the action of the other really takes place in fairyland, associated though its incidents be with hills and caves and woodlands familiar to both storyteller and audience. There was a centuries old historic convention restraining and directing the one; the other, lacking such a convention, was at the mercy of the individual storyteller.*

Another peculiarity of the later Ossianic literature—the standing antagonism between the Fenian warriors and the *Lochlannach*—is perhaps largely due to the assumed emergence of the saga under Brian and his successors. For Brian, the victor of Clontarf struck down in the moment of crowning victory, was essentially a champion of the Gael against the Gall or foreigner. What more

* Compare with this Mr. MacNeill's views discussed, Appendix, pp. 53–60.

natural than that his deeds and those of his warrior son, Murachaidh, should colour the south Irish saga once it came into the hands of the court bards or reciters? Certain it is that both father and son figure frequently in the later Ossianic romances and in folk-tales connected therewith, thus testifying to the fact that their substance goes back to a time when the valiant deeds of the Dalcassian princes were still fresh in the memory of the Irish race.

Be this as it may, and whether the explanation which I have essayed be accepted or not, it remains true that in the post twelfth-century Irish literature the Ossianic cycle occupies an almost predominant position. The oldest texts of the secondary or mediæval stage of the cycle is also the longest and in many ways the most important of all, the so-called *Agallamh na Senorach*, or *Colloquy of the Elders*. I know nothing in any literature that at all resembles it. Formally, it is a chaos of local legends connected only by the fact that all are put into the mouth of Caoilte, the last survivor of the Fenian band, and are related by him either to Patrick or to various chieftains with whom he takes up his quarters. It thus follows the model of the pre-mediæval topographical poem put in Finn's mouth, in which the mention of each place calls up its appropriate story. Like so many Irish texts the *Colloquy* is a mixture of prose and verse.

The protagonist, as already stated, is Caoilte; Ossian is, indeed, mentioned as being, save Caoilte, the sole survivor of the band, but he goes to stay with his fairy mother in the elfin mound of *Ucht Cleitigh*, whilst his comrade perambulates the length and breadth of Erin and expounds to his wondering and eager hearers the heroic lore of the past. Among these hearers none is more eager or more naïvely and intently interested than Patrick. From the time that he and his clerics meet the tall men with their huge wolf-dogs, and wonder greatly as they gaze upon them, "for the largest man among them reached but the waist or else to the shoulder, and they sitting," of the Fenian warriors, the saint's curiosity is unwearied and persisting. True he has some scruples at first. "Were it not for us an impairing of the devout life, an occasion of neglecting prayer, and of deserting converse with God, we, as we talked with thee, would feel the time pass quickly, warrior." But his two guardian angels come to reassure him, and "with equal emphasis and concordantly" urge that the ancient warriors' tales be written "on tabular staffs of poets and in minstrels' language, so that it be a pastime for the nobles of the latter time to give ear to them." The devout saint pays due heed to this message from Heaven, and the close of each incident recalled to Caoilte's memory by the sight of some hill or grave mound is marked by his approval:

"Success and benediction, Caoilte, all this is a recreation of spirit and mind to us. And where is Brogan the scribe?" Nor does his satisfaction stop short here. In the course of their wandering, Fian and saint come to the grave of a warrior who had died of shame because he could not on the spot fittingly reward a poet who had panegyrised him. "Heaven and his release from torment be from me to him in recompense of his sense of honour," is Patrick's comment, and "in that very hour his soul came out of pain and sat on Patrick in the form of a white dove." Nay, he grants Heaven to a minstrel of the fairy clan who delights him with his music; "but for a twang of the fairy spell that infests it nothing could more nearly resemble Heaven's harmony," is his remark to his scribe, and the latter's answer deserves record, "if music there be in Heaven, why should there not be on earth, wherefore it is not right to banish away minstrelsy." That Caoilte should receive Heaven as the reward of his storytelling need not surprise, but indeed he is as devout and curious of the saint's teaching as the saint is gracious and curious of his pagan lore; the relations between the two are full of an exquisite and courteous cordiality. One feels that for the storyteller to whom we owe the *Colloquy*, the glories of old time Erin were dear, but not dearer than the Heaven which by grace of Mary's son and Patrick's intercession he himself hoped one day to win.

There is no unity in the *Colloquy*, no connecting link save the personality of the narrator. Close upon a hundred legends are given in full or in brief, the latter as a rule. The allusions are often so curt and remote as to be unintelligible to us nowadays. Here, we feel, is a vast mass of legend, all more or less familiar to the storyteller's hearers, summed up in terse form. In its extant form the *Colloquy*, of which the MSS. belong to the late fourteenth and early fifteenth century, is in the main, I think, a compilation of the late thirteenth century ; if this is so, the storytellers of the previous hundred and fifty years must indeed have been busy with the Ossianic heroes, for scarce a page of the *Colloquy* but presupposes romances which must at one time have existed in a more lengthened form.

The subject-matter of the Ossianic episodes which make up the *Colloquy* is various. We find instances of the theme of an oversea princess fleeing from an abhorred husband or suitor to seek protection with those patterns of chivalry and valour, Finn and his champions ; we have raids, oversea, by Fenian warriors in search of brides or treasure. But by far a larger number of stories involve the relations between the Fenian and the fairy clan, the Tuatha de Danann. These are pictured as akin to mortals in form and stature, though gifted with more than mortal beauty and grace ; liable to violent death, but immune from disease and old age ;

brave, but less brave and warlike than the human warriors whose aid they eagerly seek in the conflicts they wage among themselves; endowed with such superhuman powers as invisibility and shape shifting, and, in especial, preeminent in magic and wizardry. Thanks to these powers they frequently take the upper hand at first, but in the long run fortune remains with the Fenian warriors, and hard though be the straits in which they often find themselves they invariably emerge with enhanced fame and the repute of unconquerable prowess. The fairy maidens are often fain of the mortal heroes; nor do the chieftains of Faery disdain to seek brides among mortal maidens. Matter is thus yielded for a number of love tales, mostly tragic in their issue, but related with a gentle pathos, lacking all ring of true passion, which is characteristic of the *Colloquy*. Akin to this is the general tone of soft melancholy which pervades the romance—it is full of lament for the days that are no more, but the lament is neither bitter nor piercing; it recognises the inexorable and weeps over it, but neither rails nor curses.

Sensitiveness to natural impressions and delight in the chase are characteristic of the *Colloquy*, as, indeed, they are of Ossianic romance in every stage of its development. Whereas the fighting pieces strike the reader as perfunctory and conventional, all that relates to woodcraft and woodland life is treated with a deep-felt joyousness. Nature, especially in her sterner moods, is keenly observed, as witness the following lay on winter—

"Cold the winter and the wind is risen; the high-couraged, unquelled stag is on foot. Bitter cold to-night is the whole mountain, yet for all that the ungovernable stag is belling. The deer of Slievecarn of the gatherings lays not his side to the ground; no less than he, the stag of frigid Echtge's summit catches the chorus of the wolves. I, Caolite, with brown Dermot and with keen light-footed Oscar, we, too, in the nipping night's waning end would listen to the music of the pack."

But the minstrel has as keen an eye for the softer aspects of nature—

"O well of the strand of the two women, lovely thy luminous branching crosses; from thy banks thy trouts are to be seen, thy wild swine in the wilderness hard by, thy fair hunting-cragland, thy deer, thy dappled and red-chested fawns . . . lovely the colour of thy purling stream, O thou that art azure-hued and green as the surrounding copsewood is mirrored in thee."

Contemporary in all probability for the most part with the *Colloquy* (though some are certainly older and others demonstrably younger) are a number of poems, mostly narrative, but some lyrical or elegiac, best known from a collection made in the early seventeenth century by Northern scribes for Captain Sorley MacDonnell of the well-known Antrim family. These are in course of publication by Mr. John MacNeill under the title *Duanaire Finn*; half of the collection has so far (1910) appeared.*

These poems which are in the strict metre of Middle Irish versification differ for the most part, in so far as may be judged from the portion already published, from the *Colloquy* as regards the subject-matter of the various episodes which they narrate. They assign a larger space to the feuds of the various clans comprised in the Fenian organisation, in particular to the feuds between the Clanna Baoisgne and the Clanna Morna; indeed several seem to represent a distinctively Connaught form of the saga, designed to exalt Goll at the expense of Finn. The Tuatha de Danann appear less prominently, the theme of monster-combat is less insisted upon. The tone of the narrative is, on the whole sterner, more realistic than that of the *Colloquy*. The *rôle* of witness is generally taken by Ossian not Caoilte, but to this there is one curious exception. We have seen (*supra*, p. 16) that in the Book of Leinster poem, Finn and the Phantoms, the story is related by Ossian disguised as Guaire the Blind. The *Duanaire* has a version of the same poem tallying closely with the older one, but ending thus: "I am

* For Contents, see p. 67.

Caoilte the beloved, left behind the faultless heroes." If one were to reason from what has taken place elsewhere in the Ossianic literature, *i.e.* the substitution of Ossian in place of Caoilte, one might conclude that the version contained in the seventeenth-century MS. belongs in reality to an earlier stage than of the twelfth-century MS., but this conclusion would hardly be warranted, as possibly only a scribal error is involved.

The relationship of saint and hero in so far as it is pictured in the *Duanaire* does not, on the whole, differ markedly from that described in the *Colloquy*, although none of these poems dwell upon it with the same complaisant sympathy. But one of the poems (No. XXX., "The Hunger of Crionloch's Church") introduces a new note—

> My curse upon thy churchmen, Patrick, and mayest thou rot! If I had Oscar, he would not leave me to hunger,

protests the hero. As we shall see, this spirit of reviling antagonism dominates large portions of the later poetry.

The *Duanaire*, as stated above, contains poems the extant form of which may differ in age by so much as three or four centuries in so far as the subject-matter is concerned; it also reveals here and there a process of decadence. Thus two poems (Nos. III. and IV.) deal with the same episode of the strife between Finn and Goll. The first, put in the mouth of Garaidh, a hero of the Clanna Morna, whilst naturally giving the chief place to Goll, yet does full justice to Finn in recounting the combat of knightly generosity between the two heroes; the second, obviously later as the editor notes, at once vilifies Finn and makes him ridiculous, and yet the *rôle* of narrator is assigned to Ossian. Such ineptitude can hardly be put down as a mere scribal error, but must be taken as exemplifying a stage of the literature in which themes and incidents were modified without regard to the genuine nature of the saga.

The *Duanaire* forms a transition to the third main division of the Ossianic literature, the post mediæval.

(*c*) Post-Mediæval Ossianic Romance.

Here the contrast with the *Colloquy* is intensified. It is as if we left a cathedral close, gracefully monotonous in its uniform hues of grey and green, touched with the high-bred air of a spot remote from earthly passion and strife, and ventured forth into a wild and rocky moorland where man, living close to Nature at her sternest, becomes stern and fierce as the tempest he dares, or the wolf he pursues. The differences concern the form and subject-matter as well as the tone and spirit of the texts. Whereas the *Colloquy* is in prose interspersed with verse, the narratives we now have to consider are almost wholly in verse. Caoilte is no longer the witness *par excellence* to the departed glories of the Fenian prince, Ossian has almost completely ousted him. Many of the personages, scenes, and incidents recorded in the *Colloquy* are absent from the ballads, in which again we find much for which the *Colloquy* affords no clue. Of infinitely greater importance is the change of tone and spirit. Caoilte and Patrick are, we have seen, friends who love and respect each other, each conscious of his worth and delighting to honour the other; the warrior accepts devoutly the teaching of the saint, and the saint rejoices to fling wide open the gates of heaven. Ossian, in the ballads, is as a rule a pagan, defiant and reckless, full of contempt and scorn for the howling clerics and their churlish low-bred deity. The Patrick with whom he has to do well deserves this scorn. The benignant and gracious gentleman of the *Colloquy*, keenly appreciative of the great-hearted generosity of the Fenian chiefs, is replaced by a sour and stupid fanatic, harping with wearisome monotony on the damnation of Finn and all his comrades; a hard taskmaster to the poor old blind giant, to whom he grudges food, and upon whom he plays shabby tricks in order to terrify him into acceptance of Christianity. To milder arguments indeed

Ossian is deaf; when Patrick vaunts his God as maker of field and grass and all creation the warrior answers scornfully—

'Twas not in forming fields or grass
That my King took delight;
But in mangling the bodies of heroes,
In contesting kingdoms and spreading his fame.

He cannot believe that aught could ever have resisted his father and comrades—

O Patrick, 'twas not in the time of the Fians
That that man God lived ;
Certain if he were east or west
The Fians would have stricken off his head.

Or again, in a verse which reaches the high-water mark of his indomitable and confident paganism—

Were my son Oscar and God
Hand to hand on the hill of the Fians,
If I saw my son down,
I'd say that God was a strong man.

Akin to this spirit of harsh and scornful defiance is the bitter resentment displayed by the pagan warrior as his memory recalls the days of his youth. He is old and feeble and blind, the delights of the chase and of love are denied him; these things are hard to bear, but the causes of his resentment lie deeper. He cannot away with the new world of which the Christian cleric is the symbol and the embodiment; he loathes the ascetic, churlish ideal unworthy a warrior and a gentleman, and he contrasts it with the delights that were once his, with the joy of a life wholly simple and unsophisticated, finding perfect satisfaction in battle, woodcraft and dalliance. He never wavers in his loyalty to the past; if his comrades are in hell, he is content to be there likewise. 'Would God,' he asks, 'admit his dog to Heaven's court?' And he cannot understand the Saint's indignant protest—were *he* but acquainted with God he would surely reconcile Him with the hound.

The earliest examples we have of these later Ossianic ballads are contained in a MS. compiled by James Macgregor, Dean of Lismore in Perthshire, some time before the year 1518 and thus antedating by over a hundred years the formation of the *Duanaire* collection, although the poems of the latter belong, on the whole, to an earlier stage of composition. The Dean, a lover of song and tale, jotted down all that took his fancy, poems ascribed to the heroes of the cycle, poems formally assigned to bards of his own or a slightly earlier time, some complete, some fragmentary, some a mere jumble of heterogeneous scraps. The note I have characterised in the preceding pages is firmly struck in several of the Ossianic poems in the Dean's collection. If we put aside this Scotch-Gaelic MS., which represents a tradition as old as the fifteenth century at the latest, we must come down to the seventeenth century before we find either in Scotland or Ireland MS. containing this species of ballad. But throughout the eighteenth century and in Ireland, at least, down to the middle of this century, such MSS. abound, and numberless episodes of the cycle are worked up in the form of a dialogue between Ossian and Patrick in which the railing lament of the aged warrior is a standing feature.

The literary problem disclosed by these facts has scarce been noted, still less has any serious attempt at its solution been essayed. Is the pagan, anti-clerical note of Ossianic literature younger in fact, as it is undoubtedly younger in record, than the harmony of Christian hagiology and native saga revealed in the *Colloquy of the Elders?* Did a change come over the feeling of Gaeldom at some time during the fourteenth and fifteenth centuries, originating a new conception and presentment of the relation between Saint and Pagan hero? Did this change of feeling originate in Scotch Gaeldom and did it work back to Ireland? Is it possibly due to a larger admixture of Norse blood in Scotch Gaeldom? Or is the mood, only fully revealed in the latest MSS. and in living tradition, the primitive and genuine one, and is the harmonising process noticeable in the *Colloquy of the Elders* the work of an original artist who transformed current tradition to suit the needs of an imagination at once devout and patriotic? If this later view be accepted may not the emergence of the older Pagan spirit in the later romances be due to the fact that, under the increasing competition of Classic, French and English literature from the fifteenth century onwards, the native literature fell more into the hands of the folk and thus reverted to the archaic stage from which it had started?

I am content to ask afresh these questions which no one has asked before me, and shall not essay any answer. I will merely say that whilst I concede the possibility of the anti-clerical Pagan spirit of Ossianic legend being a creation of the last four centuries, I deem it extremely improbable.

I have laid special emphasis on this one point both because it concerns the dominant feature of post-mediæval Ossianic romances, and because of its bearing upon the intellectual and moral history of the Gael alike in Ireland and in Scotland; but it must not be supposed that the note of protest and defiance, although the most characteristic, is the sole one of the later literature, and that this consists, formally, of nothing save wrangles between Patrick and Ossian. The older tradition which made Caoilte the representative of the Fenian band has not entirely disappeared from the later texts, nor, where Ossian has taken Caoilte's place, is the former always pictured as in bitter enmity with St. Patrick. Moreover, besides the dramatic narrative poems, in which the dialogue framework is of as much moment as the episode which it enshrines, many narrative poems exist which lack the framework altogether, or in which it is mere conventional ornament; there also exists a great mass of prose narratives which dispense entirely with what may be styled the "survivor" machinery, and relate episodes of the cycle in a style and tone which differ greatly from those of the poems.

These later prose romances may be roughly divided into two main classes: the first wearing a more historic aspect, selecting its themes chiefly from the relations of Finn to professed contemporaries mentioned in the annals, elaborating an account of the organisation of the Fenian band, and, as a rule, serious in intent and effect, though frequently fantastic in presentment and bombastic in style; the second humorous, almost grotesque, in choice of incident and mode of narration, or else conceived in a vein of avowed and deliberate romanticism. In this second class coincidences of incident and situation with the later stage of Arthurian romance occur not infrequently, coincidences so marked as to render improbable their attribution to chance or to essential kinship between the two bodies of literature, and to warrant the conclusion that the Franco-English romance of chivalry found its way to Ireland in the fifteenth and sixteenth centuries, and exercised some influence upon the later Ossianic tales, an influence, be it noted, secondary and accidental rather than primary and essential. Irish mythic romance reveals no trace of such deep and far-reaching modification as befell, for instance, the French *chansons de geste* after their contact with the *Matière de Bretagne*, the Arthur romances.

The humorous and grotesque stories of the second class present most affinity with the prose narratives preserved orally to this day in Ireland and Scotland; and the comparison between the MS. version, two or three centuries old, and the living folk-tale, is often of extreme interest. As a rule the folk versions are wilder, ruggeder, more fantastic than those found in MSS. of the last three centuries. It may happen, too, that the tale picked up but a few years ago has a mode of depicting the material conditions of the saga, and a method of characterisation which *look* (I do not say which *are*) more archaic than those of the MS. versions. Some scholars have urged that the tales found in MSS. of the sixteenth, seventeenth, and eighteenth centuries are inventions of the storytellers of the day, and that in percolating through to the folk they put off much of the finery with which the professional storyteller had adorned them, and put on a homely, barbaric garb. To my mind the reverse process is a more likely one: the folk were at all times full of stories about Finn and his braves, stories which, lacking either pseudo-history or highly developed literary form were taken up by the professional narrators and ultimately transcribed in the fashion of the time. This I believe was the usual course, though the other may have been, and in some cases certainly was, taken. For storyteller and audience were separated by no such gulf as divides the modern man of letters from the vast mass of the reading public. The same body of tradition was common to both, and the differences in handling, though numerous, were unessential.

Down to the middle of last century the Ossianic cycle retained its sway over the native literary class; the tales were continually being re-worked over and remodelled, and a certain amount of fresh invention, on the lines and in accord with the spirit of the older legend, took place. Thus the well-known poem of Ossian in Tir na n-Og (the Land of Youth) is undoubtedly the composition of the eighteenth-century poet Michael Comyn. But it would, I believe, be an entire mistake to imagine that he invented the central incident, or even a large amount of the subsidiary detail; he took a traditional theme and narrated it in the traditional spirit, in perfect because unconscious accord with all the conventions of the literature to which he was adding a monument. He probably knew the countryside versions, he was certainly familiar with what poets of the previous centuries had composed, and, himself the last of a long line of folk-singers, he produced a work which, his in its wording, is yet traditional and popular in substance and form.

The points in which Ossianic literature of the last four centuries, whether in prose or verse, whether collected from the lips of the folk or recorded in the MS. of the professional narrator, differs from the mediæval and pre-mediæval literature are trifling and insignificant compared with the essential similarities of matter and treatment. Development there has been, variation also; not infrequently decadence, but it still remains the same body of heroic-mythic romance, the outlines of which are clearly apparent in the twelfth-century vellums. Due stress has already been laid upon the permanence of the note of lament and protest. The theme of Fenian relation to oversea invaders, whether it assume the shape of defence against raids, of harrying expeditions to distant lands, of succour to distressed foreign damsels, or of abduction of outland brides, is constant and manifold in its variety; it forms the staple of the lengthiest prose narrative of the cycle (saving the *Colloquy*), the *Battle of Ventry*, in which Finn's *rôle* as the representative defender of Gaeldom against the foreigner culminates. Equally prominent is the theme of the Magic Hunt, in the course of which the heroes fall into the power of the wizard and fairy clan, whence they invariably escape with increase of fame. The story of Grainne's love for Diarmaid maintained its sway and found expression both in prose and verse. Scattered episodes have come down to us in fourteenth- and fifteenth-century MSS., but, as a whole, we only know it in seventeenth- and eighteenth-century versions, the very popularity of which probably tended to the disappearance of the earlier forms. The atmosphere of somewhat unreal romance is preserved to the last. Were it not for the ever-insistent delight in the wild life of woodland and mountain, we should seem to move wholly in a company of mists and phantoms. The breath of open-air life, the joy in nature, sweeten and quicken what would otherwise be too frequently tedious and inane.

It would be vain, as may be gathered from the foregoing characterisation of this literature as a whole, to seek from it a realistic representation of the life of a given period, least of all of the period in which its heroes are alleged to have lived. Its oldest texts cannot be used as evidence to pre Christian modes of life in Ireland as can the Ulster hero legends. Where precision of statement exists—as, for instance, in the elaborate account of the way in which the Fenian bands were organised and recruited, and of the rights and privileges they enjoyed—it is, I believe, wholly unreliable, the figment of a later age. It has been urged with much ingenuity that this account preserves the memory of primitive contact between Ireland and Romanised Britain, and that the military system it discloses was modelled at second or third hand upon the Roman legion. I can only avow my scepticism. The essential characteristics of Fenian organisation as pictured in the romances, are independence alike of the High King and of the Provincial Kings, and wardenship of the coasts against oversea attacks. Had any knowledge of the Roman military system penetrated to third-century Ireland it might have been used by some ambitious chief for the purpose of subjugating his neighbours; it could not have originated the idea of a national system of defence, which presupposes lasting and repeated attacks affecting the whole nation. Nothing of the kind is known in third-century Ireland. In the ninth century the state of affairs was different: hardly a district of Ireland but was affected by the Norse incursions. It is conceivable that under these circumstances some form of organised militia should spring up, independent of the tribal system, and placing its services at the disposal of any tribal chief who was specially menaced and whose ordinary resources were insufficient to meet the menace. But the account of the Fian band can hardly be taken seriously even if we suppose it to apply to facts and events of the ninth instead of the third century. It is too obviously a fancy picture, traced by some bard whose vision of the distant past was undisturbed by much real knowledge. It is none the less of extreme interest as embodying an ideal of patriotic chivalry which may be as old as the twelfth century, but probably took shape in the following century. The individual Fian must be at once an expert athlete and warrior and a poet versed in the twelve books of poetry; he must practise generosity largely, denying meat and valuables to none; he must hold his ground against any number of opponents less than nine. Collectively, the body stood outside the strict tribal rules which governed the rest of Irishmen: "if their guarantee was violated they must not accept material compensation in satisfaction." As a rule, if any Irishman was injured his tribe was bound to exact material compensation, the extent and nature of which were rigidly determined. As satisfaction was generally denied, private grievances became tribal feuds, and tribal enmities which prevented any effectual combination against the foreign invader were perpetuated. Some loosening of tribal ties way well have taken place in the ninth-century warrior bands, the prototype of the Fenian militia described in the mediæval texts, and in so far there may be an historical basis for the mediæval account.

In other respects there is scarce a trace in the Ossianic stories of the sharply bitten, highly elaborate description of the material life and circumstances of the chieftain-warrior class which makes the texts of the Ulster cycle of such inestimable value to the student of the past. The descriptions of Finn's household and retainers which, it is true, have been preserved, lack the realistic precision of the earlier cycle. But the very feeling that continually besets the reader of this literature, the feeling that the storyteller is projecting himself back into a golden age which he knows to be unreal, enhances its value as an expression of the ideals which haunted the mind of the bardic storytellers and their audience of chiefs and warriors. Courage, magnanimity, boundless generosity—these, the last especially—are the proper attributes of the heroes

> Were but the brown leaf which the wood sheds from it gold,
> Were but the white billow silver,
> Finn would have given it all away !

—is Caoilte's proud vaunt of his dead lord. Indeed, so perpetual is the insistence upon the virtue of open-handedness as to warrant the surmise that the storyteller class no longer possessed the assured standing of earlier times, and was compelled to stimulate the liberality of its patrons. As the hero is a free giver, so also he must have a free mind, hating what is false, and crooked and mean :

We the Fians never told a lie,
Falsehood was never known to them;
'Twas by truth and the might of our arms
We 'scaped unhurt from each conflict.

And again:

Patrick, 'twas not the wont of the Fians
Not to give choice of the fight to their foes;
Treachery they cherished not, nor malice,
Not such was the repute of their tribe.

Perhaps the finest picture of the warrior chief as conceived by the idealising fancy of mediæval Gaeldom is to be found in the two panegyrics upon Finn and Goll preserved by the Dean of Lismore:

Both poet and chief,
Braver than kings,
Firm chief of the Fian.

. . .

Foremost always,
Generous, just,
Despising a lie.
Of vigorous deeds,
First in song.
A righteous judge,
Firm in rule.

. .

Marble his skin,
The rose his cheek,
Blue was his eye,
His hair like gold.
All men's trust,
Of noble mind.

Of ready deeds,
To women mild.

. . .

Noblest of kings,
Finn ne'er refused
To any man,
Howe'er unknown.
Ne'er from his house
Sent those who came.

Or again:

A hero brave,
Bold in assault.
His bounty free,
Fierce to destroy.
Beloved of all,
Goll, gentle, brave.

. . .

Skilful and just
He rules his men,
His bounty wide,
A bloody man.
First in the schools,
Of gentle blood
And noble race,
Liberal, kind,
Untired in fight,
No prince so wise.

. . .

Leopard in fight,
Fierce as a hound,
Of women loved.

What, it may be asked, is the literary merit of this body of romance? I have quoted enough, I trust, to show, even in an English dress, the frequent charm and beauty of detail. That it does not as a whole reach a very high level is due to the fact that it is essentially a mass of fairy tales, lacking that firm grip upon the elemental realities and passions possessed by all really great literature. The fairy tale, when it comes straight from the heart of a gifted and unsophisticated race, may often possess a direct, and naïve beauty that is irresistible; or again, if it fall into the hands of an artist endowed with the temperament to feel and the skill to render its charm, it may assume a shape of alluring loveliness. Instances of both kinds of beauty occur in Ossianic romance, but, as a whole, when it came into the hand of the literary, the storytelling class in Ireland, that class no longer attracted, if I mistake not, the most gifted minds of the race. Thus no single passage or episode in the Fenian cycle is as representative of native Gaelic artistry at its highest as much that may be cited from the Ulster sagas. Moreover, whilst the storytelling class which elaborated the Ossianic romances possessed conventions of narrative and expression which it diversified with extreme ingenuity, it did not renew them, deprived as it was of really fertilising contact with other literatures. The result was that the inherent weaknesses of all fairy-tale romance were developed rather than removed, and the greater part of the Ossianic cycle is a literature of decadence in so far as it is rooted in the past and not in the present, and is compelled to derive its sustenance from convention and not from contact with life. Certain characteristics of the language in which the romances are composed further tend to accentuate defects from which romance at its best is never free. Gaelic is a language of extraordinary richness of vocabulary and variety of expression. Handled by generation after generation of literary artists, who sought novelty in ever-fresh elaboration of style rather than in invention of incident or revivification of spirit, it tends to fall at last to the level of the merely ingenious and pretty. All English translators of Ossianic poetry have dwelt upon the difficulty of a faithful rendering which shall avoid monotony and tedium. The same things are apparently being said over and over again. In English, yes; not so in Gaelic, where the wealth of synonym enables the poet to repeat himself with a slight variation. It thus comes to be the artist's aim to find many and varied expressions of an idea rather than to seek the only right one. In realistic literature, contact with life will often produce adequate expression, even if artistic skill be lacking, but in romance the finest feeling is required for what alone is truly adequate in selection and rendering of incident. The dialogues between Patrick and Ossian contain matter promising in the extreme, but there was lacking an artist capable of conceiving all that the contrast of ascetic Christianity and Pagan joy of life implied, and of seeking until he found the one form of words adequate to the conception.

A word or two must be said upon a point that was fiercely debated between Ireland and Scotland after the publication of Macpherson's poem—the relative share of either section of Gaeldom in the Ossianic legend. The debate was futile because those who carried it on lacked the historical sense. They lost sight of the fact that up to the fifteenth century certainly, and, to a large extent, even during the seventeenth and part of the eighteenth century, Gaeldom, from a literary point of view, was practically one. The Gael of Ireland and Scotland shared equally in a common body of romance. This fact was forgotten by the Irishman and Scotchman of a hundred years ago, who, overlooking the romantic character of the cycle and dwelling solely upon its connection with historic fact, claimed it as a record, however distorted, of the past history of their land. The Irishman had far more reason on his side, because the historic basis such as it is of the cycle is connected with Gaelic Ireland and not with Gaelic Scotland; he was wrong in not recognising that much of the incident contained in the cycle has just as much claim to be localised in Gaelic Scotland as in Gaelic

Ireland, or indeed wherever the Gael might have settled when he was still in the mythopœic stage, because it is no reflection, however distorted, of actual fact, but a translation into the terms of heroic romance of older mythic material common to all Gaels. He was also wrong in not recognising that the Scotch Gael was justified in developing this common body of romance in his own way, and that the specific Scotch Gaelic developments have exercise a marked, and in some cases, I would urge, a beneficial, effect upon the cycle as a whole. The Scotch disputants, on the other hand, put themselves out of court by their denial that Ireland was the land in which took place the historic events of the cycle, and in which it first assumed a literary shape which reacted upon and profoundly modified the popular versions. I have called the dispute futile, but it was not wholly so: in the ardour of debate texts were printed and criticised, and much valuable material was thus brought to light which might otherwise have remained hidden. But at this time of day the old controversy should be allowed to die and Irish and Scotch Gaels should unite in cherishing the Ossianic romance as a common possession to be cared for and studied with brotherly emulation.

Dr. Hyde has already called attention to the fact that the metrical revolution which transformed Gaelic poetry in the seventeenth and eighteenth century—ultimately sweeping away the intricate system of metrics which had been in force since the tenth century at least—seems to have originated in Scotch Gaeldom. I have hinted at the possibility that the tone and spirit of the later Ossianic ballads may be a specific Scotch Gaelic creation. I would dwell for one moment upon one characteristic feature of Ossianic romance, its fondness for certain aspects of nature, as that also seems to me connected with Scotland. When the late Mr. Black celebrated with unwearied iteration the beauty of the Western Isles of Scotland, he was, all unknown to himself, taking up a tradition that had been potent among the Gaelic minstrels for over a thousand years. The gem of mediæval Gaelic nature poetry, indeed of all nature poetry written in any European vernacular for over a thousand years, is Deirdre's farewell to Alba in the *Woe of the Sons of Usnech.* The following from the *Colloquy* has not the poignant charm of that exquisite lament, but it gives a vivid impression of the joyous woodland outdoor life in which the Fenian heroes delighted—

> Arran of the many stags, the sea impinges upon her shoulders!
> An isle in which whole companies were fed, and with crags among which blue spears are reddened.
> Skittish deer are on her pinnacles, soft blackberries on her waving heather; cool water there is in her rivers and mast upon her russet oaks.

Greyhounds there were in her and beagles; blackberries and sloes of the dark blackthorn; dwellings with their backs set close against her woods, while the deer fed scattered by her oaken thickets!

A crimson crop grew on her rocks, in all her glades a faultless grass. Over her crags, affording friendly refuge, leaping went on, and fawns were skipping!

Smooth were her level spots, fat her wild swine, cheerful her fields . . . her mast hung on the boughs of her forest hazels, and there was sailing of long galleys past her.

Right pleasant their condition all when fair weather sets in! Under her river banks trouts lie; the seagulls whirling round the grand cliff answer one the other. At every fitting time delectable is Arran!

It may well be that minute and loving descriptions such as these are due to men sprung from the isles and glens they picture so fondly.

It is hard in so few pages to give an adequate account of a literature which has lived for so many centuries, and which still lives in the heart and memoryof many thousand Gaelic-speaking peasants. The note of permanence, of continuity, is indeed the crowning wonder of Ossianic romance, and may well be emphasised afresh by way of conclusion to this brief study. If an English minstrel from the court of Canute or the Confessor revisited the world he would—granting the initial difficulty of language were overcome—find scarce a hundred living men who could follow his recitation with any measure of understanding. To the most learned of scholars much would be entirely obscure, much only partially followed; to the vast mass of educated Englishmen his songs and stories would be meaningless, crowded with personages, incidents, and themes wholly unfamiliar. A French minstrel of the same period would stand a better chance; from the Universities of France, Germany, and Italy might be drawn an audience fairly familiar with the subject-matter of his lays, whilst the man of average education would at least have a bowing acquaintance with Charlemagne and his Peers. But if a contemporary of Brian Boru were to appear in many districts of Ireland or the Highlands, and tell his tales of Finn and the Fians, subject-matter, mode of narration, methods of description and characterisation—all would appeal familiarly to his audience of peasants ignorant for the most part of reading or writing. Storytellers and hearers alike would praise the generosity and wisdom of Finn, celebrate the fleetness of Caoilte, the irresistible beauty of Diarmaid, the rude prowess of Goll; alike they would mourn the untimely fate of Oscar, bravest of the brave. The tales of Finn's birth and upbringing, of Ossian's fairy parentage, of Grainne's tragic love, would find hearers as appreciative, as familiar with every detail as when the minstrel recited them at the court of the Dalacassian princes. Here and there narrator and hearers would find differences; each would note the appearance of unfamiliar heroes and adventures; the narrator might be found old-fashioned, or he, again, might condemn the modern versions as diffuse and tasteless. But these points of difference would be unimportant, and scarce affect the startling conclusion that well-nigh the same stories as were told of Finn and his warrior braves by the Gael of the eleventh century, are told in well-nigh the same way by his descendant of to-day.

The Historic Background of the Ossianic Saga according to Mr. J. MacNeill.

In his introduction to the *Duanaire Finn*, Mr. MacNeill has propounded a new theory of the historical and racial conditions which gave rise to the Ossianic literature, and were largely influential in determining its evolution.

Up to now the *crux* of the Ossianic problem has been the disagreement between the historical and political conditions described in the literature and those known to us from annals and other texts of a more or less historical character. The Ossianic texts speak of bands of warriors independent of the tribal organisations which culminated in the kingships associated in the North with Tara, in the South with Cashel. The function of these warrior bands is to defend Ireland against oversea aggressors, the chiefs of these bands occupy a privileged position, treat on almost equal terms with the High King (at that time the king at Tara), with whom they are allied by marriage.

A priori there is nothing to be said against the possibility of such bands having existed, but it is evident that, as an indispensable pre-requisite of their existence, Ireland must have been exposed to violent and persistent attacks against which the tribal organisation was powerless, and which called in being a new military body. But at the time assigned to Fenian bands, roughly speaking, the 2nd–3rd centuries A.D., Ireland was, it is almost certain, entirely free from oversea aggressors. Southern Britain was, as a whole, under Roman sway, and the Roman authorities had no intention of engaging in a forward policy against Ireland.[7] As far as Northern Britain is concerned, so far from its being a centre of aggression against Ireland, it was exposed to invasion and immigration from Ireland. Nothing, again, outside the Ossianic texts, represents the Kings of Tara at this period as weak rulers unable to cope with their enemies, foreign or native, and compelled to accept the compromising assistance of an independent military organisation; on the contrary, the Northern Kings of what may be styled roughly the Ossianic period (covering the lives of Cumhal and his son Finn), are the most famous and powerful of Irish historic legends, Conn the Hundred-Fighter who gave its designation, Conn's half, to the Northern part of the island, and his grandson Cormac, a typical saga-king comparable, *mutatis mutandis*, with Arthur, Dietrich or Charlemagne. The historical *données* of the Ossianic texts are incompatible with those of remaining Irish literature dealing with the same period.

I have accepted, on the whole, in the foregoing pages the current explanation of this incompatibility, namely, that the "history" such as it is of the Ossianic texts does not reflect the condition of the third but of the ninth century (*supra*, pp. 8–11). Mr. MacNeill's explanation is different. For him the picture of the 2nd–3rd century Tara and Cashel Kings as it is found in annalistic and other texts of the eighth to eleventh centuries is a fancy one; these Kings were not possessors of a long established power, descendants of a long line of ancestors reaching far back beyond the Christian era. They were, on the contrary, the warrior inaugurators of Irish polity as known to us throughout the mediæval period; they extended their sway over Ireland precisely because they went outside the tribal organisation of their Aryan Celtic kinsmen, because (like the English in India) they formed the fighting, non-Celtic peoples, they subdued into a sort of standing army, subject (as the Celtic tribesmen were *not* subject) to permanent military service. The Fenian bands of the Ossianic texts reflect, in howsoever distorted a form, the machinery thanks to which Conn in the North, Eoghan (Mogh Nuadat) in the South established the Milesian kingships of Tara and Cashel. The Ossianic saga belongs originally to one of these fighting, non-Milesian subject peoples. The historic thread upon which the incidents of the saga (themselves of older, mythic nature) are strung is the record of blood-feuds between rival clans, feuds with which the Tara kings had nothing to do.

The development postulated by Mr. MacNeill is briefly as follows: By the seventh to eighth century the Milesian organisation was firmly established all over Ireland; the distinction (which in theory was still maintained by the Irish antiquaries down to the seventeenth century) between the governing Milesians and the subject peoples had, in practice, been obliterated. The time was ripe for the admission of the hero tales dear to the subject populations into the official *corpus* of Irish storytelling, but for this it had to be freed from all "servile" taint, its protagonists had to be dignified by contact with the Milesian ruling clan; Finn's antagonist must be no less a person than Cormac himself; the final destruction of the Fenian heroes must involve the death of Cairbre, Cormac's son. The process thus postulated was a slow one; centuries were required before the prejudices of the Milesian storytelling class (a class, be it noted, enjoying high official status, subject to arduous professional discipline, and to which were assigned duties only less important than those of the chieftain class), were overcome, before Finn could take place as a Gaelic hero beside the Cuchulinn whom the conquering Milesians of the second and third century had annexed from the older Ulidians. In the course of those centuries the Norse invasions took place and profoundly modified the Ossianic saga still in a state of flux. The knowledge of the true nature of the subject-races militia had died away with the gradual amalgamation of Milesians and non-Milesians although the existence of such a militia bulked too largely in the saga for it to be overlooked; naturally, therefore, it came to be explained by conditions familiar to the storytellers, the conditions of the ninth century during which every coast of Ireland knew the perpetual menace of oversea attack.

It would be no wonder, on Mr. MacNeill's showing, if every extant Ossianic text betrayed evidence of Milesian contamination as such contamination may have begun as early as the late seventh century and our oldest paleographic witness to the cycle does not reach back beyond the mid-eighth century. But he claims that one text has come down to us free of contamination. The instance is instructive. In the *enfances* of Finn we have the variant of a widespread heroic theme known as the "Expulsion-and-Return formula." In the eleventh century MS., the Book of the Dun Cow, is a tale entitled, "The Cause of the Battle of Cnucha." In this the story of Finn's begetting and boyhood is related as sober history, rationalistically, and involving the antagonism of Finn's kin and the Tara rulers. But there exists another version of the same events, which is found in a fifteenth-century MS. and is entitled Finn's Boyish Exploits (*Macgnímartha Finn*). Here is no feud of Cumhal and the Tara Kings; the hero is slain by the Luagni and the House of Morna, and it is upon them that the hero's son, Finn, must wreak vengeance. Mr. MacNeill regards the *Macgnímartha* (which professes to be transcribed from a now lost MS., the Psalter of Cashel, probably compiled in the time of Cormac of Cashel, slain in 908) as a survival of the pre-Milesian Stage of Ossianic literature.

Mr. MacNeill's whole Introduction should be carefully studied, but I have said enough I trust to show its importance and how its acceptance would modify our conception of the cycle as a whole. I may say that whilst the existence of the names, Conn's half and Mogha's half for North and South Ireland does support the contention that these chieftains are the standard bearing representatives of a revolutionary settlement of Ireland, I find it almost impossible to reconcile the postulated revolution with what we know of third-century Irish history. Where did the Milesian conquering settlers come from? certainly not from outside Ireland. Secondly, I find the complete ignoring of this subject-race militia by all Irish literature, save *ex hypothesi* the Ossianic texts inexplicable; nor, indeed, can I explain its disappearance. The fourth-century Irish, as we know from the native tales of Niall and from the Roman accounts of the harrying Scots, were an aggressive, invading, settling people; surely the organisation forged during the period of internal conquest would have persisted, nay, have been developed in that of external conquest. Nor, thirdly, when we consider what a race of fighters were the early Irish as revealed in the Ulidian epics the heroes of which are perpetually on the war path, can I easily accept a view which regards liability to military service as the token of "servile" status.

On the other hand I fully accept Mr. MacNeill's dating for the *Macgnimartha*. When I first studied this tale thirty years ago * I pointed out that it is essentially more archaic than the eleventh-century Battle of Cnucha. But I do not think recognition of this fact necessarily implies all that Mr. MacNeill claims. I note that other very early

* The Aryan Expulsion-and-Return formula in the Folk-and-Hero Tales of the Celts (*Folk-Lore Record*, vol. iv.).

testimonia to Ossianic story (*e.g.* the Finn-Mongan connection, and the reference to the Diarmaid-Grainne love tale) involve " Milesian " traits.

The future will show if Mr. MacNeill's ingenious theory is correct. If so a study, such as the foregoing, should undoubtedly start from the discrimination of Milesian and non-Milesian elements, and should consider the whole development of the Ossianic literature in the light of the mutual relations of these two elements.

CHRONOLOGICAL APPENDIX

SECOND AND THIRD CENTURY, A.D.—Period of the Fenian warriors.

According to the Irish Annals Cumhal, Finn's father, was uncle to Conn the Hundred fighter, high king of Ireland, whose death is recorded by the Four Masters in 157 A.D. Art, father of Finn's father-in-law, Cormac, was slain in the Battle of Magh Mucruimhe, recorded by the Four Masters in 195 A.D.; the first year of Cormac's reign is placed by them in 227 A.D., his death in 266 A.D. They record Finn's death in 283 A.D., following the eleventh-century annalist, Tighernach. But Tighernach's contemporary, Gilla Caemhain, makes Finn die fifty-seven years after Magh Mucruimhe, which, if his date for that battle be the same as Tighernach's, a fact that cannot now be ascertained, would place it in 252 A.D. Tighernach, followed by Four Masters, ascribes the Battle of Gabhra to the year 284 A.D. He mentions Cairbre's death, but makes his slayer Seniach, son of Fer Cirb of the Fothairt. Cormac, Cairbre and Finn are the only personages of the saga mentioned by Tighernach, who represents the strict historical point of view; his silence concerning other personages and incidents of the cycle warrants the conclusion that he looked upon them as belonging to romance rather than to history, but does not justify doubt concerning the existence of the romances in his day; he was equally reticent as regards the Ulster cycle, with the monuments of which he must of course have been perfectly familiar.

FIFTH CENTURY.—Apostolate of Patrick, whose death is recorded, by the Four Masters in 493 A.D.

EIGHTH CENTURY.—The tales about Mongan-Finn, preserved in the Book of the Dun Cow, possibly belong to the latter part of the century. They seem to antedate any trace of Norse influence and to be very little later than the Voyage of Bran, which is almost certainly a composition of the early eighth century at the latest.

NINTH CENTURY.—The Norse invasions, which began at the close of the eighth century, and continued throughout the ninth century, profoundly affected the Ossianic cycle as a whole. Indeed, Professor H. Zimmer has gone so far as to deny altogether the alleged third century historic basis of the cycle and to assert that the historical Finn was the ninth century chief of a mercenary band—half Norse, half Irish. I have given a full summary of his argument in the Introduction to Campbell's *Fians*. It will suffice here to say that, whilst Professor Zimmer's insistence upon the important Norse element in the Ossianic tales is fully recognised, his theory as to the personages of the cycle has entirely failed of acceptance.

EARLY TENTH CENTURY.—Cormac, the King Bishop of Cashel, was slain in 908. A glossary of words and expressions, obsolete in his day, has come down to us containing many very important quotations from works now lost. Whilst it is doubtful if the glossary is actually to be attributed to him, it is almost certain that it is only a little younger in date. The oldest portion of the glossary contains references to and stories about Finn.

The *Amra Choluimb Chille*, the Elegy upon Columba traditionally ascribed to Dallan Forgall, the sixth- and seventh-century bard, is, according to Professor J. Strachan (*Revue Celtique*, xvii., 41 *et seq.*), a composition of the early ninth century. The glosses upon this poem preserved in the Book of the Dun Cow are probably a century younger. These glosses have preserved the verse of a poem celebrating Grainne's love for Diarmaid. See *supra*, p. 18, and *infra*, p. 70. The *Amra* was edited and translated by Dr. Whitley Stokes in the *Revue Celtique* vol. xx. (1899), when for the first time this remarkable monument of early Irish scholastic literature was made really accessible to the student, not the least among the many invaluable services which Dr. Stokes rendered to Irish studies.

LATE TENTH AND EARLY ELEVENTH CENTURIES.—Rise to power of the Munster chieftain Brian of the Dalg Cais, slain in 1014 at Clontarf. Throughout the eleventh century the Dalcassian princes and their bards and learned men are prominent. All the stories about Finn found in the Book of the Dun Cow *must* have been compiled before 1050, and probably represent a mass of written tradition already one hundred to one hundred and fifty years old.

LATE ELEVENTH CENTURY.—The Book of the Dun Cow was copied from earlier MSS., before 1106, when its scribe was slain. Professor H. Zimmer has argued with great plausibility that it is a transcript of MSS. collected and revised by Flann of Monasterboice, who died in 1054 with the reputation of being the most learned man of his day.

EARLY TWELFTH CENTURY.—The last Norse invasion of Ireland took place under Magnus Barelegs (so nicknamed by his Norse subjects from his fondness for the Irish dress), slain in 1103. This invasion has left its trace in the Ossianic post-mediæval ballad of Manus, and is, apparently, the last historic event which has affected the cycle.

MID-TWELFTH CENTURY.—The Book of Leinster was compiled in the years preceding 1160 It is largely made up of transcripts from much earlier MSS., but it also contains poems by almost contemporary writers.

THIRTEENTH CENTURY.—Probable date of redaction of the *Colloquy of the Elders* preserved in MSS. of the fourteenth and fifteenth centuries. It should be noted, however, that whilst the *Colloquy* is full of traces of Norse influence, it is, apparently, altogether free from any traces of the Norman invasion.

FOURTEENTH CENTURY.—Probable date of some of the poems contained in the *Duanaire Finn*. Two of these contain references to the Normans in the guise of prophesies.

LATE FIFTEENTH CENTURY.—Latest possible date for the Ballad literature in semi-dramatic form vouched for by the Book of the Dean of Lismore, compiled in the years preceding 1518.

EARLY SEVENTEENTH CENTURY.—The Duanaire Finn, the oldest existing Irish-Gaelic MS. of Ossianic post-mediæval ballads, was copied in 1627 from earlier MSS., the transcript being made for a Captain Sorley MacDonell of the great Antrim family. This collection is being edited by Mr. Eoin MacNeill. Vol. i. appeared in 1906. I have dealt with the Introduction, *supra*, pp. 53–60. Probably all the poems antedate the MS. by at least a hundred years, the majority by two or three centuries.

MID-EIGHTEENTH CENTURY.—Composition of the poem Oisin in Tir na n-Og, by Michael Comyn, probably the last deliberate bit of creation or rearrangement of the legendary substance of the cycle.

About the same time James Macpherson was composing his Ossian in Scotland. But whereas Comyn remains perfectly faithful to the traditional subject-matter and mode of presentment, Macpherson disregards the latter entirely and the former very largely.

BIBLIOGRAPHICAL APPENDIX

I first cite the chief works in which Ossianic literature may be found printed, and to which constant reference has been made in the foregoing pages. I then go through the study, page by page, and append notes upon any points likely to be of use to the student.

Miss Brooke.—Reliques of Irish Poetry, &c., Dublin, 1789.

Contents: Conloch and Cucullan. Magnus the Great. The Chase. Moira Borb. War Ode to Osgur. Ode to Gaul, &c. (the remaining contents are non Ossianic). The texts edited and translated by Miss Brooke belong to the post-mediæval section of Ossianic literature.

Oss. Soc.—Transactions of the Ossianic Society for the years 1853–58, 6 vols., Dublin, 1854–1861.

Contents: Vol. I.—The Battle of Gabhra. Vol. II.—The Festivities at the House of Conan of Ceann-Sleibhe. Vol. III.—The Pursuit after Diarmaid O'Duibhne and Grainne, edited by Standish Hayes O'Grady. How Cormac mac Airt got his Branch. The Lamentation of Oisin after the Fenians. Vol. IV.—Fenian Poems edited by John O'Daly: the Dialogue between Oisin and Patrick: Battle of Cnoc an Air. The Lay of Meargach. The wife of Meargach. The Chase of Loch Lein. The Lay of Oisin on the Land of Youth (Comyn's poem edited by Bryan O'Looney). The Boyish Exploits of Finn (fifteenth-century text edited by J. O'Donovan). Vol. V.—The Proceedings of the Great Bardic Institution, edited by O. Connellan (not an Ossianic text). Vol. VI.—Fenian Poems edited by John O'Daly: the Chase of Sliabh Guilleann. The Chase of Sliabh Fuaid. The Chase of

Gleann an Smoil. The Praise of Beinn Eadair. The Hunt of Sliabh Truim. The Chase of Sliabh na-m-Ban. The Chase of the Enchanted Pigs of Aenghus an Brogha. The Hunt on the Borders of Lough Derg. The Adventures of the Amadan Mor.

Simpson.—Poems of Oisin, Bard of Erin, &c., by J. H. Simpson, London, 1857.

Contents: Deardra. Conloch. Dialogue between Oisin and St. Patrick (with summaries of the same Poems as in Oss. Soc. IV.). Oisin comes from the Youthful City. Conversion of Oisin. Fionn goes to Graffee. Fionn goes to Loughlin. Enchantment of the Giants in Ceash. Oisin born of a doe. Death of Erraran son of Fionn. A Grecian Princess comes to Erin. The Battle of Ventry Harbour.

A valuable collection made in Munster and South Connaught.

Lismore.—The Dean of Lismore's Book, &c., edited by the Rev. Th. McLauchlan. Edinburgh, 1861.

Contains twenty-eight Ossianic pieces.

Leabhar na Feinne.—Heroic Gaelic Ballads collected in Scotland chiefly from 1512 to 1871, arranged by J. F. Campbell. London, 1871.

Prints the Ossianic portions of the Book of the Dean of Lismore, the Dunstaffnage MS. (1603), the Ardchonail MS. (1670), and the collections of Pope, MacNicol, Jerome Stone, Fletcher, MacDiarmaid, Kennedy, Gillies, Irvine, Turner, MacCallum, and smaller collections of the eighteenth century as well as Campbell's own collections. The Gaelic text alone is given, but Kennedy's English summaries are printed.

Silva Gadelica.—A collection of Tales in Irish, edited and translated by Standish Hayes O'Grady. London, 1892.

Contains the following Ossianic pieces: X.—The Panegyric of Cormac and the Death of Finn, son of Cumhall.

XI.—Enumeration of Finn's Household. XII.—The Colloquy of the Ancients (my quotations in the foregoing pages are made from this fine version). XVIII.—Pursuit and Flight of the Gilla Decair. XIX.—The Carle in the Drab Coat. XXI.—The Enchanted Cave of Ceshcorran. XXVI.—The little Brawl at Almhain.

Mr. O'Grady's translation of the Colloquy is made from the Book of Lismore (an Irish fifteenth-century MS. not to be confounded with the Scotch Book of the Dean of Lismore), which is imperfect in many places. Dr. Whitley-Stokes has printed the missing portions from the Oxford MS. in Irische Texte, vol. iv. part i.

Campbell. Fians.—Stories, Poems and Traditions of Fionn and his Warrior Band, collected from oral sources by J. G. Campbell. London, 1891.

Forms Vol. IV. of Waifs and Strays of Celtic Tradition. Mr. Campbell, Minister of Tiree, must not be confounded with J. F. Campbell, of Islay, the collector of the West Highland Popular Tales.

Mr. Campbell's Fians, collected in Tiree within the last thirty years, afford wonderful proof of the vitality of the Ossianic cycle among the Gaelic speaking peasantry. In the bibliographical notes to the volume, I have given the concordance of the versions with the older Irish sources as far as known, and with the versions contained in the Leabhar na Feinne. These notes thus form a rough index to the larger part of the cycle.

Duanaire Finn.—The Book of the Lays of Fionn. Part I. Irish Text, with translation into English by Eoin MacNeill. I.—Contents : The Abduction of Eargna. II.—Fionn's Foray to Tara. III.—The Rowan Tree of Clonfert. IV.—The Battle of Cronnmhóin. V.—The bathing of Oisín's head. VI.—The Foray at Loch Luig. VII.—Caoilte's Mischief Making. VIII.—The Crane Bag. IX.—Goll's Malediction. X.—Goll's parting with his wife. XI.—The Kindred of Fionn. XII.—The Household of Almha. XIII. — The Headless Phantom. XIV.—The Enchanted Stag. XV.—The Boyhood of Fionn. XVI.—The Shield of Fionn. XVII.—Caoilte's Urn. XVIII.—The Daughter of Diarmaid. XIX.—Lament for the Fiana. XX. — The Sword of Oscar. XXI.—The Battle of the Sheaves. XXII.—The Death of Goll. XXIII.—The Adventure of the Men from Sorcha. XXIV.—The Chase of Sliabh Truim. XXV.–XXXII. — Short elegiac fragments. XXXIII. — The Sleep Song for Diarmaid. XXXIV.—Fionn's Prophesy. XXXV.—The War-Vaunt of Goll.

Revue Celtique.—Vols. I–XXX. Paris, 1870—1910.

The following Ossianic pieces are contained in this admirable periodical, which first under the editorship of Mons. Henri Gaidoz, then under that of Mons. D'Arbois de Jubainville, has rendered more services to the study of Celtic antiquity than any other publication of its kind.

I.—Fionn's Enchantment (J. F. Campbell). II.—The Battle of Cnucha (from the Book of the Dun Cow, W. M. Hennessy). V.—Macgnímartha Find (Kuno Meyer). VII.—Finn and the Phantoms (from the Book of Leinster. Whitley Stokes). XI.—Uath Beinne Etair (from Harl, 5280, K. Meyer). XIII.—L. C. Stern, Le MS. irlandais de Leide (a fifteenth-century MS. which contains some interesting Ossianic texts, which are given in the original and in a French translation). Oscar au fléau (Douglas Hyde). The Battle of Mag Mucrime (Whitley Stokes). XIV.—Two tales about Finn (from the thirteenth-century MS. Stowe 992, Kuno Meyer).

Ventry.—Cath Finntrága, or the Battle of Ventry, edited from MS. Rawl. B. 487, by Kuno Meyer. Oxford, 1885.

Edited from the same fifteenth-century MS. which contains the oldest text of the *Colloquy*, after which this is the longest of all the Fenian Romances. The editor's Introductions are of great interest and value.

NOTES

PAGE 1. *Macpherson.*

The latest and most authoritative work is Mr. J. S. Smart's *James Macpherson (Ossian): a literary episode*, 1905 (3*s*. 6*d*.) The best brief summary of the debate with which I am acquainted is contained in Mr. A. Macbain's articles, Macpherson's Ossian, *Celtic Magazine*, Feb.–April, 1887. The *Report of the Highland Committee*, 3 vols, 1805, is still worth consulting.

PAGE 9. *The Battle of Gabhra.*

The oldest text relating to this battle, a poem of seven quatrains, placed in Ossian's mouth preserved in the Book of Leinster, has been edited and translated by E. O'Curry, *Oss. Soc.*, i. pp. 49–57.

PAGES 11–15. *The Pre-Mediæval Ossianic Romance.*

I have collected all the references accessible at the time, (1890) in my Essay on the development of the Fenian or Ossianic saga: *Waifs and Strays*, vol. ii. *Cf.* pp. 402–408.

The tales about Mongan-Finn are edited and translated by Prof. Kuno Meyer, *Voyage of Bran*, vol. i. pp. 42 *et seq.*

The poem *Finn and the Phantoms* is translated and edited by Dr. Whitley Stokes *Revue Celtique*, vol. vii. pp. 289 *et seq.* A later text in Dunanaire Finn. A Highland folk-tale which presents the most marked analogies to the early poem has been edited and translated by Campbell of Islay, *Revue Celtique*, vol. i. pp. 193 *et seq.*

PAGE 13. *Finn's Poem on Winter.*

I have translated Professor Zimmer's German version (*Kelt. Beiträge*, III,) correcting by Dr. Whitley Stokes' version in his edition of the *Amra Ch. Chille*. It is also edited and translated by Prof. K. Meyer, *Four Old Irish Songs of Summer and Winter*, 1903 (2*s*.)

PAGE 14. *The Cairn Incident.*

This is found in one of the most archaic of Irish heroic legends: The Destruction of Daderga's fort, which relates how Conaire Mor, high-king of Ireland, was surprised and slain by piratical raiders. Before starting to attack the fort they pile up a cairn. The whole tale has been edited and translated by Dr. Whitley Stokes.

PAGE 17. *Diarmaid and Grainne.*

The great story list in the Book of Leinster (printed in O'Curry's MS. Materials, pp. 583–593) has preserved the title of a story, *Aithed Grainne re Diarmait*, the main outlines of which were almost certainly the same as in the extant version. The Book of Leinster story list is undoubtedly as old as the early eleventh, and may be as old as the early eighth, century. The tale in its present form, is edited and translated by Mr. Standish Hayes O'Grady (*Oss. Soc.*, vol. iii.) from eighteenth-century MSS. What is apparently a fragment of an earlier recension has been edited and translated by Professor Kuno Meyer (Uath Beinne Etair) from a fifteenth-century MS. Harl. 5280, *Revue Celt.*, vol. xi.

In addition to the verse quoted on p. 18 the commentary to the *Amra Ch. Chille* contains another fragment, two lines of a speech addressed by Diarmaid to Grainne, vaunting the woodland fare he can offer her. See Dr. Stokes' translation, *Revue Celt.*, vol. xx.

In the Arthurian romance the story of Guinevere's love for Lancelot, which is at least as old as the year 1160, has probably replaced a much older and ruder version. Guinevere's infidelity is alluded to by Geoffrey of Monmouth.

An interesting feature of the Diarmaid-Grainne story is its association with the rude stone monuments. All over Ireland cromlechs are found known as Diarmaid and Grainne's beds. This has been held to denote an archaic strain in the story.

PAGE 20. *The Dalcassian Princes and their Court.*

Among the works which almost certainly were composed in Munster may be mentioned the history of the struggles between the Irish and Norsemen: *The Wars of the Gaedhil with the Gaill*, edited and translated by Todd, 1862. It is also probable that the extant recension of the Book of Rights is of Munster origin. The chief poet of the Dalcassian court was Mac Liag, who died in 1015.

Brian and Murachaidh (Murrogh) appear as folk-tale heroes very early. In ch. xcviii. of the *Wars of the Gaedhil* a dialogue is recorded between Dunlang O'Hartugan and Murachaidh in which the latter speaks of the allurements held out to him in "elf-mounds and fairy mansions." Although this chapter is, as Todd says (p. clxxviii. 5), an evident interpolation in the eleventh-century work, it must nevertheless be at least as old as the fourteenth century, as it is found in Todd's MS. D. which he assigns to that century. The scene of the famous folk-tale, the Leeching of Cian's Leg, is placed at Brian's Court. The earliest known recension is edited and translated, *Silva Gadelica* (No. xx.), from a fifteenth-century MS. The oral versions (Cf. *Waifs and Strays*, vol. ii., pp. 208 *et seq.*) are much fuller, and, I believe, represent an earlier stage of the tale than the fifteenth-century MS.

PAGE 21. *The Norsemen in the Ossianic Stories.*

Professor Rhys contends (*Hibbert Lectures*, p. 355) that the Norsemen (Lochlannach) have taken the place of earlier mythical adversaries of Finn, and that "Lochlann, like the Welsh Llychlyn, before it came to mean the home of the Norsemen, denoted a mysterious country in the lochs and seas."

PAGE 24. *Grave-opening.*

A common *motif* in the *Colloquy* is the opening of a Fenian warrior's grave and the rifling of its treasures. Eight such instances occur in the Book of Lismore version. I cannot help connecting this feature with the well-known grave-rifling practices of the Norse invaders.

PAGE 25. *The Tuatha de Danann.*

For a full discussion of the nature and attributes of this mysterious race I would refer to my *Voyage of Bran*, in particular to chapters xvii. and xviii., and to Popular Studies, No. 7. *The Fairy Mythology of Shakespeare.*

PAGE 26. *The Woodland Note in the Ossianic Romances.*

This note is absent from the tales of the Ulster heroic cycles, excepting the *Woe of the Sons of Usnech*, which in this, as in other respects, shows affinity with the Fenian cycle. It should also be noted that it is prominent in the Arthurian cycle, especially in romances connected with Tristan and Gawain. Until the Ossianic romances have been studied much more carefully it would be premature to found any argument of date upon this characteristic. It *may* denote that the stories belong to a very archaic stage as it *may* also be simply a trait which the Ossianic shares in common with other branches of mediæval literature.

PAGE 32. *The Lament for Past Days.*

As I have pointed out in my Introduction to Campbell's *Fians*, this note, characteristic of one of the great cycles of Gaelic romance, can be paralleled in Brythonic (Welsh romance. There exist in Welsh a number of poems, attributed to the sixth-century Llywarch Hen, which picture him as the last survivor of the heroic struggle against the invading Saxons, lamenting his youthful prowess and joy of life. Whilst these poems cannot be, as once was thought, the composition of the sixth-century chieftain, they are at least as old as the eleventh century. The tone of Llywarch Hen, like that of the Ballad Ossian is bitter and resentful.

PAGES 31–32. *The Ballad Ossian.*

Quite adequate acquaintance with this section of post-mediæval Ossianic literature can be obtained from (*a*. as regards Scotland) the *Book of the Dean of Lismore*, Ian Campbell's *Popular Tales*, and *Leabhar na Feinne*, and J. G. Campbell's *Fians ;* (*b*. as regards Ireland) from the Ossianic Society publications, and from Simpson. I may refer again to my bibliographical notes to Campbell's *Fians* as supplying a summary index to the chief themes and episodes.

I should note that I use the term *ballad* in default of a short term of a more precise nature. The Ossianic narrative poems are not *ballads* in the sense we apply to the word, and the genuine ballad is almost unknown in Gaelic literature.

PAGE 36. *Pseudo-Historic Stories in the Later Ossianic Literature.*

The numerous late versions of the tale found in the Book of the Dun Cow, The Cause of the Battle of Cnucha may be cited as representative specimens.

PAGE 37. *Romantic and Humorous Prose Stories in the Later Ossianic Literature.*

Examples may be found in *Silva Gadelica* (No. xvii. The Flight and Pursuit of the Gilla Decair; No. xix. The Carle of the Drab Coat; No. xii. The Enchanted Cave of Keshcorran), and Joyce, *Old Celtic Romances* (The Fairy Palace of the Quicken Trees; The Pursuit of the Gilla Dacker). The romantic type is represented by the Battle of Ventry.

PAGE 37. *Ossianic Folk-Tales.*

Numerous examples may be found (*a.* for Scotland) in Campbell of Islay's *Popular Tales*, in McInnes' *Folk and Hero Tales* (Waifs and Strays, vol. ii.), in MacDougall's *Folk- and Hero-Tales* (Waifs and Strays, vol. iii.), and in Campbell's *Fians;* (*b.* for Ireland) in Larminie's *West Irish Folk-Tales*, 1894, 6*s.*; in Curtin's *Hero-Tales of Ireland* (1895, 8*s.* 6*d.*), and *Myths and Folk-Lore of Ireland* (1890, 9*s.*)

The question of the relations between the Irish MS. and the oral folk-versions has been discussed by myself in the introductions and notes to the various volumes of *Waifs and Strays of Celtic Tradition*, more especially in the Introduction to vol. ii. MacDougall's *Folk- and Hero-Tales* and by Dr. Hyde and myself in the Introduction to the former's *Beside the Fire.*

PAGE 42. *The Qualifications of a Fenian Warrior.*

The earliest extant text is that edited and translated *Silva Gadelica* (No. x.) from a fifteenth-century MS. As Dr. Hyde notes it is couched in a vein of true Celtic hyperbole (*Lit. Hist. of Ireland*, p. 373). It is much as if we found a series of rules for an All England Eleven, admission to which was made conditional upon the applicant's scoring 1000 runs per innings, and bowling the opposite eleven with consecutive balls.

Page 49. *Scotch Origin of the Metrical Revolution.*

Cf. Dr. Hyde's *Literary History of Ireland*, ch. xxxix. Dr. Hyde finds the earliest trace of the new system in the poems of Mary, daughter of Alaster Rua MacLeod, born in 1569.

I may fittingly close with a few words of advice to students who wish to advance the interpretation of the Ossianic legend by original work. Very much remains to be done before we can form a clear idea of their origin, nature, and development, and even without a knowledge of Gaelic, much assistance may be rendered by any one willing to take a little trouble. Thus, a careful comparison of the subject-matter of the cycle as presented in the *Colloquy*, in the *Duanaire*, and in the later recorded *ballads*, cannot fail to throw much light upon the problems involved, as would also comparison of the specific Scotch and Irish forms of the *ballads*. But, of course, such comparisons are likely to be far more fruitful if made by Gaelic students. The majority of the Ossianic texts have come down to us in a form differing but slightly from the spoken language, whether in Ireland or Scotland; they are thus accessible to any one who knows the spoken language. At the some time these texts are, to a very large extent, remodellings of much earlier ones, they preserve many archaic words, constructions, and traces of early metrics, and thus afford an excellent bridge to the study of the mediæval literature. Moreover, they offer by far the best means of following the differentiation of Irish-Scotch Gaelic which has taken place within the last four centuries.

A number of interesting points offer themselves for investigation: the *dramatis personæ* of the cycle, their names, attributes, body of incidents with which they are specially connected; the *locale* of the cycle, the way in which it has been adapted to various districts of Gaeldom;

the historic basis of the cycle, the way in which it has affected or been affected by the traditional romantic element; the specific relation of the Irish and Scotch versions; the specific relation of the prose and poetic versions and the determination of their respective ages by linguistic tests; the metrical system of the poems and its relation to mediæval Irish metrics; the presence of dialectic traits in the texts, &c.

It is only by detailed investigations such as these that the foundations can be laid for a real history of Irish romantic literature. I sincerely trust the foregoing pages will not only induce a certain number of students, whether Gael or Cymry or English, to take up the work of investigation for themselves, but will also be found of some assistance to them, at all events at first.

Printed by Ballantyne & Co. Limited
Tavistock Street, Covent Garden, London

Works for the
Ossianic Cycle

Published by David Nutt

James Macpherson (Ossian): a Literary Study. By James S. Smart. Crown 8vo. 1905. 3/6 net.

*** The most searching and scholarly examination of the various questions connected with Macpherson's work. Whilst doing full justice to his literary merit, Mr. Smart conclusively marshalls the arguments against Macpherson's authenticity, and shows that the sources of his inspiration are largely those of contemporary English literature.

The Fians, or, Stories, Poems and Traditions of Fionn and his Warrior Band, collected from oral sources, by the Rev. J. G. Campbell of Tiree. With Introduction and Bibliographical Notes. By Alfred Nutt. Demy 8vo. 1891. 7/6 net.

*** *See* p. 67.

Duanaire Finn. The Book of the Lays of Fionn. Irish Text with translation into English by Ewin MacNeill, and historio-critical Introduction. Demy 8vo. 1908. 10/6 net.

*** *See* the present study *passim*.

CPSIA information can be obtained
at www.ICGtesting.com
Printed in the USA
LVOW03s1407220817
545939LV00021B/1589/P

9 781314 295269